STATE PROFILES

NEW YORK

BY ALICIA Z. KLEPEIS

BLASTOFF!
DISCOVERY

BELLWETHER MEDIA • MINNEAPOLIS, MN

Blastoff! Discovery launches a new mission: reading to learn. Filled with facts and features, each book offers you an exciting new world to explore!

BLASTOFF! UNIVERSE

BLASTOFF! Beginners — GRADE K

BLASTOFF! READERS — GRADES 1-3

BLASTOFF! DISCOVERY — GRADE 4

This edition first published in 2022 by Bellwether Media, Inc.

No part of this publication may be reproduced in whole or in part without written permission of the publisher.
For information regarding permission, write to Bellwether Media, Inc., Attention: Permissions Department,
6012 Blue Circle Drive, Minnetonka, MN 55343.

Library of Congress Cataloging-in-Publication Data

Names: Klepeis, Alicia, 1971- author.
Title: New York / by Alicia Z. Klepeis.
Description: Minneapolis, MN : Bellwether Media, Inc., 2022. |
Series: Blastoff! Discovery: State profiles | Includes bibliographical references and index. | Audience: Ages 7-13 | Audience: Grades 4-6 | Summary: "Engaging images accompany information about New York. The combination of high-interest subject matter and narrative text is intended for students in grades 3 through 8"– Provided by publisher.
Identifiers: LCCN 2021021392 (print) | LCCN 2021021393 (ebook) | ISBN 9781644873373 (library binding) | ISBN 9781648341809 (ebook)
Subjects: LCSH: New York (State)–Juvenile literature.
Classification: LCC F119.3 .K55 2022 (print) | LCC F119.3 (ebook) | DDC 974.7–dc23
LC record available at https://lccn.loc.gov/2021021392
LC ebook record available at https://lccn.loc.gov/2021021393

Editor: Rebecca Sabelko   Designer: Brittany McIntosh

Printed in the United States of America, North Mankato, MN.

TABLE OF CONTENTS

VIEW FROM PANTHER MOUNTAIN
ADIRONDACK PARK

A warm summer day welcomes a family to Adirondack Park. They visit the Wild Center in the village of Tupper Lake. First, they check out the Center's otter pups and wood turtles. Later, they explore the Wild Walk. A bald eagle soars past as they climb along this series of elevated bridges in the treetops.

EMPIRE STATE BUILDING

LETCHWORTH STATE PARK

STATUE OF LIBERTY

THOUSAND ISLANDS

The family finishes lunch and sets their sights on Panther Mountain. Tall pines tower over them on the trail. A cottontail rabbit darts into the bushes. They climb a small ridge, then enjoy an incredible view from the summit. Welcome to New York!

New York is in the northeastern United States. It covers 54,555 square miles (141,297 square kilometers). The state capital is Albany. It sits along the Hudson River in the east. The state's biggest city is New York City. Buffalo and Rochester are other large cities.

New York's northern land neighbor is Canada. They are separated by Lake Ontario and the St. Lawrence River. New York's eastern neighbors are Vermont, Massachusetts, and Connecticut. In the southeast, part of New York is surrounded by the Atlantic Ocean. New Jersey and Pennsylvania lie to the south. The waters of Lake Erie and the Niagara River splash against New York's western edge.

BUFFALO

LAKE
ERIE

N
W E
S

CANADA

ST. LAWRENCE RIVER

VERMONT

LAKE ONTARIO

ROCHESTER

SYRACUSE

NEW YORK

ALBANY

MASSACHUSETTS

HUDSON RIVER

CONNECTICUT

PENNSYLVANIA

NEW YORK CITY

LONG ISLAND

LONG ISLAND

Long Island lies at the southeastern tip of New York. This island is about 118 miles (190 kilometers) long. But it has more people than all but 12 of the U.S. states!

NEW JERSEY

ATLANTIC OCEAN

7

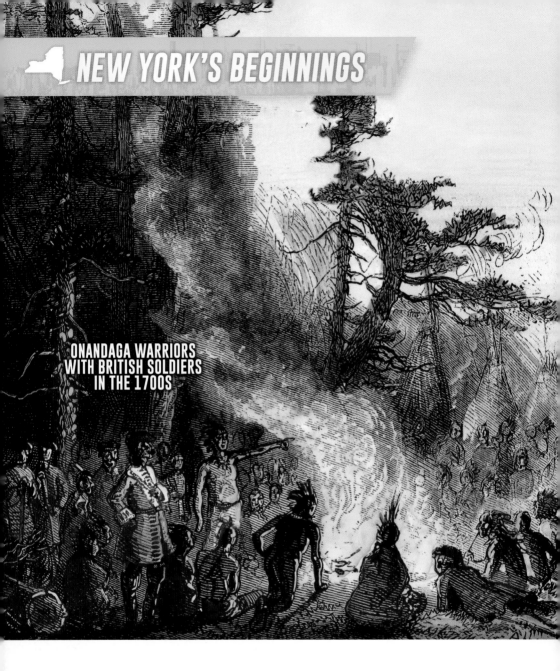

NEW YORK'S BEGINNINGS

ONANDAGA WARRIORS WITH BRITISH SOLDIERS IN THE 1700S

Present-day New York has been home to people for thousands of years. Over time, people formed groups within the Algonquian language family and the Iroquois **Confederacy**. Many tribes made up each group. They were farmers, hunters, and gatherers.

Europeans may have explored the area as early as 1524. Dutch people permanently **settled** there in 1624. They founded a **colony** called New Netherland. English settlers also arrived in the 17th century. New York became the 11th U.S. state in 1788.

NATIVE PEOPLES OF NEW YORK

New York has 8 federally recognized Native American tribes and 3 state-recognized tribes. There are 11 reservations within the state's borders.

ONEIDA

- Original lands in central New York
- Around 15 Oneida people live on the Oneida Nation Reservation in New York today

ONONDAGA

- Original lands south of Syracuse, New York
- More than 150 Onondaga people live on the Onondaga Nation Reservation in New York today

CAYUGA

- Original lands include areas surrounding Cayuga Lake
- Nearly 3,000 Cayuga people live on the Cayuga Nation tribal area today

SAINT REGIS MOHAWK

- Original lands in northeastern New York
- More than 3,000 Mohawk people live on the Saint Regis Mohawk Reservation today

The Adirondack Mountains cover most of northern New York. The area is home to lakes, waterfalls, and dense forests. The Mohawk River flows through central New York. It joins the Hudson River in the east. Lowlands along the **Great Lakes** rise into the Allegheny **Plateau** in southern New York. In the southeast, the Atlantic Coastal **Plain** includes the islands within the Atlantic Ocean.

HUDSON RIVER

MOHAWK RIVER

N
W E
S

ADIRONDACK MOUNTAINS
ALLEGHENY PLATEAU
ATLANTIC COASTAL PLAIN

NEW YORK'S FUTURE: SEA LEVEL RISE

Global sea levels are rising due in part to climate change. Some estimate that sea levels along New York's coastline will be up to 6 feet (2 meters) higher by 2100. This could create many problems for the state's heavily populated coastal areas.

LONG ISLAND
ATLANTIC COASTAL PLAIN

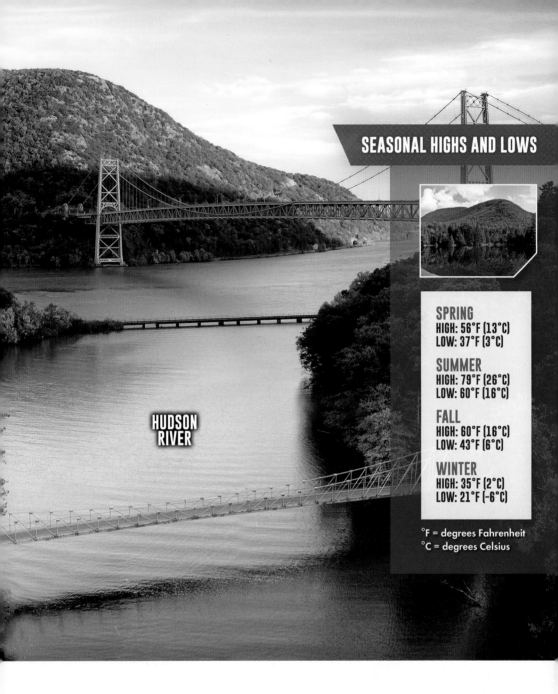

HUDSON RIVER

SPRING
HIGH: 56°F (13°C)
LOW: 37°F (3°C)

SUMMER
HIGH: 79°F (26°C)
LOW: 60°F (16°C)

FALL
HIGH: 60°F (16°C)
LOW: 43°F (6°C)

WINTER
HIGH: 35°F (2°C)
LOW: 21°F (-6°C)

°F = degrees Fahrenheit
°C = degrees Celsius

New York's climate varies from season to season. Winters are cold and often snowy. Syracuse, Buffalo, and Rochester are among the snowiest cities in the U.S. Summers can be **humid** and warm. **Precipitation** falls throughout the year.

11

WILDLIFE

NORTH AMERICAN PORCUPINE

NORTHERN FLYING SQUIRREL

COMMON SNAPPING TURTLE

New York is home to many kinds of animals. Red-tailed hawks soar above marshes. They search for muskrats hiding amongst reeds. Red-spotted newts and mink frogs dwell in moist habitats.

Bobcats prey on rabbits and white-tailed deer in the mountainous parts of the state. Porcupines chomp on leaves and fruit in the St. Lawrence River valley. Flying squirrels glide from tree to tree. Great horned owls perch on the edges of fields. Bluebirds, Canada geese, and bobolinks are also found throughout the state.

EASTERN BLUEBIRD

SUPER SNAPPERS

The snapping turtle is the New York state reptile. It has no teeth, but its bite is strong enough to remove a finger!

RED-SPOTTED
NEWT

Life Span: up to 15 years
Status: least concern

red-spotted newt range =

LEAST CONCERN	NEAR THREATENED	VULNERABLE	ENDANGERED	CRITICALLY ENDANGERED	EXTINCT IN THE WILD	EXTINCT

Over 20 million people live in New York. Most New Yorkers dwell in cities and towns. More than two out of five people live in New York City. Other **hubs** are Buffalo, Rochester, and Syracuse.

BUFFALO

FAMOUS NEW YORKER

Name: Alicia Keys
Born: January 25, 1981
Hometown: New York, New York
Famous For: Award-winning musician, actor, and judge on the TV show *The Voice*

The majority of New Yorkers have European **heritage**. Hispanic Americans and Black or African Americans make up the next-largest groups. Nearly 1 in 10 people is Asian American. Almost one-quarter of New Yorkers are **immigrants**.

Many come from the Dominican Republic, China, Mexico, Jamaica, and India. Native Americans make up fewer than 1 out of 100 people in New York.

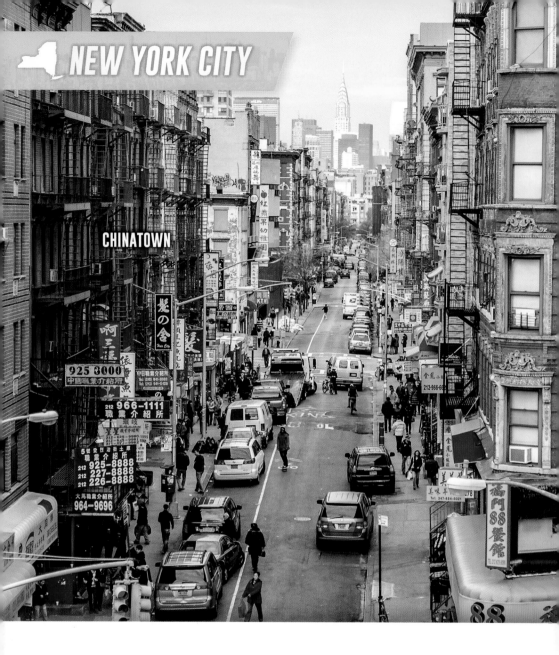

CHINATOWN

Dutch settlers first arrived in what is now New York City in 1624. The city grew into an important trade center. The development of the city's five **boroughs** began in the late 1800s. Today, New York City has many **ethnic** neighborhoods. Some include Chinatown, Little Italy, and Little Dominican Republic.

There are hundreds of **cultures** across the city. A visitor to Chinatown might eat pork buns. Buckwheat noodles are a favorite from Little Tokyo. The green space of Central Park offers New Yorkers a place to escape the city's bustle. People can enjoy an amazing city view from the Empire State Building.

CENTRAL PARK

TIMES SQUARE

Over 50 million tourists visit Times Square each year. Its bright lights and exciting energy draw visitors from around the world.

NEW YORK'S CHALLENGE: JOB CREATION

Since April 2019, millions of New Yorkers have lost their jobs. Service jobs have seen the largest drop in employment. Experts think it may take years to create jobs in New York.

FARMERS MARKET
NEW YORK CITY

Trade and farming were common ways for New Yorkers to make a living during the colonial era. Both transportation and **manufacturing** became more important to the state's economy in the 1800s. Today, factories in New York make chemicals, computer products, and medical instruments. New York farms produce dairy products, fruits and vegetables, and eggs.

Most people in New York have **service jobs**. Some work in the finance or **insurance** industries. Others have government or real estate jobs. Technology is a growing field across the state. **Tourism** also employs many people.

INVENTED IN NEW YORK

MODERN AIR CONDITIONING

Date Invented: 1902

Inventor: Willis Haviland Carrier

JELL-O

Date Invented: 1897

Inventor: Pearle B. Wait

SCRABBLE

Date Invented: 1933

Inventor: Alfred Mosher Butts

SERRATED KNIFE

Date Invented: 1919

Inventor: Joseph Burns

BUFFALO WINGS

New York's food options are as varied as its people. Food trucks in New York City offer falafel, hot dogs, Mongolian barbecue, and Belgian waffles. Buffalo wings are wildly popular and were invented in Buffalo. Tomato pie is a well-loved version of pizza in Utica. Tomato sauce and grated cheese top soft pizza dough.

Seafood is commonly eaten along the coastline. Locally produced apples are used in cider, pies, and apple butter. Cheesecake is a famous dessert, especially in New York City. Black and white cookies are also a favorite of New Yorkers.

FALAFEL

TOMATO PIE

EGG CREAM

1 SERVING

This sweet and fizzy drink has been popular in New York City for over a century.

INGREDIENTS
1/2 cup seltzer water
1/2 cup milk
chocolate syrup, to taste

DIRECTIONS
1. Pour the seltzer into the glass first, or it may bubble out of the glass.
2. Pour in the milk, then stir in the chocolate syrup until dissolved. Enjoy!

NIAGARA FALLS

Millions of people visit Niagara Falls State Park every year. The falls are over 176 feet (54 meters) high in some places. A boat called *Maid of the Mist* takes people close to the falls.

Boating and fishing are popular activities in New York's waters. Long Island's beaches are busy each summer. Hikers hit the trails year-round in state parks. New Yorkers ski and snowboard on Gore Mountain in winter. The state is home to many professional sports teams. Major League Baseball's New York Yankees have an especially huge following.

LONG ISLAND

People from around the world travel to New York City to see Broadway shows. Visitors to Cooperstown head to the National Baseball Hall of Fame and Museum. The Color Factory and the Benjamin Gallery feature the artwork of famous and up-and-coming artists.

BROADWAY

NOTABLE SPORTS TEAM

New York Yankees
Sport: Major League Baseball
Started: 1903
Place of Play: Yankee Stadium

NEW YEAR'S CELEBRATION

New York City is the site of one of the world's most famous New Year's Eve celebrations. A giant crystal-covered ball falls over Times Square just before midnight. Fireworks and a colorful parade are part of the city's Lunar New Year in January or February. People also eat fish, sweet rice balls, and noodles during this holiday.

Spring flowers are the focus of Rochester's Lilac Festival and Albany's Tulip Festival. The New York State Fair takes place each summer. It includes outdoor concerts, farm exhibits, and exciting rides. New Yorkers celebrate their state and its rich culture throughout the year!

BIG, BOLD BALLOONS

The Macy's Day Parade is a New York City Thanksgiving tradition that began in 1924. The parade's huge balloons often include popular cartoon characters!

1524

Italian explorer Giovanni da Verrazzano arrives in the area that is now New York

1664

After five years of disagreements, the British take control over the Dutch colony and rename it New York

1825

The Erie Canal opens, creating a faster way to move goods between the Great Lakes and New York City and opening up the settlement of northern New York

1624

The first permanent European settlement in the area is created by the Dutch in present-day Albany

1788

New York becomes the 11th state in the U.S.

1886

The Statue of Liberty is built in New York Harbor

1929

The New York Stock Exchange crashes, contributing to the Great Depression

2001

A terrorist attack destroys New York City's World Trade Center towers in an event that becomes known as 9/11

2020

New York City is an early center of the COVID-19 pandemic, which leads to the shutdown of many businesses and thousands of deaths across the state

1964

The Harlem riot begins after the police-related death of James Powell, a Black teenager

2008

David Patterson becomes the first African American governor of New York

Nickname: The Empire State

Motto: *Excelsior* (Ever Upward)

Date of Statehood: July 26, 1788 (the 11th state)

Capital City: Albany

Other Major Cities: New York City, Buffalo, Rochester, Syracuse

Area: 54,555 square miles (141,297 square kilometers);
New York is the 27th largest state.

Population
20,201,249
(2020)

STATE FLAG

The flag of New York is dark blue. The state's coat of arms is in the center.
It features the sun rising over a mountain. It also shows a ship and a sailboat
on the Hudson River. A bald eagle sits on top of a globe. It symbolizes
freedom and strength. The women beside the coat of arms stand for Liberty
and Justice. The state motto is below the coat of arms inside a white ribbon.

INDUSTRY

Main Exports

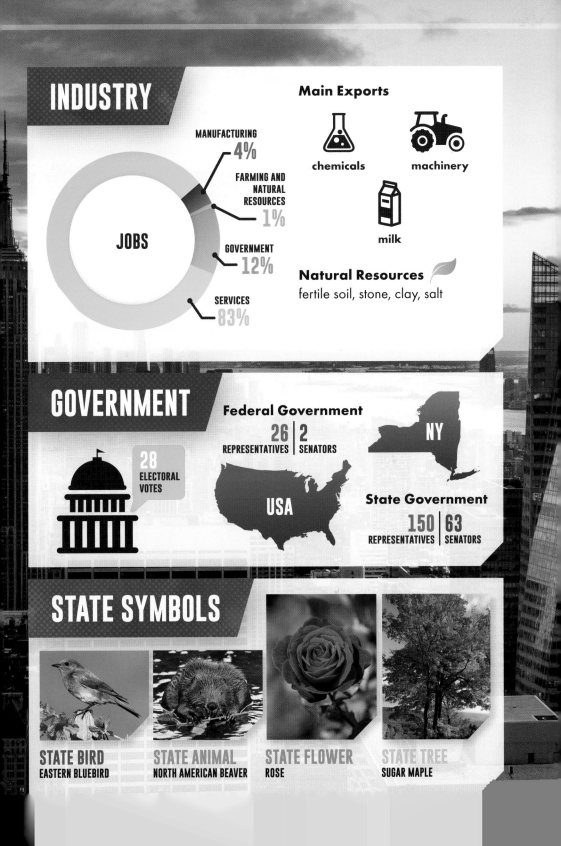

chemicals

machinery

milk

JOBS

MANUFACTURING
4%

FARMING AND NATURAL RESOURCES
1%

GOVERNMENT
12%

SERVICES
83%

Natural Resources
fertile soil, stone, clay, salt

GOVERNMENT

Federal Government
26 REPRESENTATIVES | **2** SENATORS

28 ELECTORAL VOTES

USA

NY

State Government
150 REPRESENTATIVES | **63** SENATORS

STATE SYMBOLS

STATE BIRD
EASTERN BLUEBIRD

STATE ANIMAL
NORTH AMERICAN BEAVER

STATE FLOWER
ROSE

STATE TREE
SUGAR MAPLE

GLOSSARY

boroughs—the five divisions of New York City; the boroughs include the Bronx, Brooklyn, Manhattan, Queens, and Staten Island.

colony—a distant territory which is under the control of another nation

confederacy—a union between people, states, or parties

cultures—the beliefs, arts, and ways of life in places or societies

ethnic—related to a group of people who share customs and an identity

Great Lakes—large freshwater lakes on the border between Canada and the United States; the Great Lakes are Superior, Michigan, Ontario, Erie, and Huron.

heritage—the traditions, achievements, and beliefs that are part of the history of a group of people

hubs—centers of activity

humid—having a lot of moisture in the air

immigrants—people who move to a new country

insurance—a business in which people pay money for protection against injuries or damages

manufacturing—a field of work in which people use machines to make products

plain—a large area of flat land

plateau—an area of flat, raised land

precipitation—water that falls to the earth as rain, snow, sleet, mist, or hail

service jobs—jobs that perform tasks for people or businesses

settled—moved somewhere and made it home

tourism—the business of people traveling to visit other places

TO LEARN MORE

AT THE LIBRARY

Keranen, Rachel, Dan Elish, and Stephanie Fitzgerald. *New York: The Empire State*. New York, N.Y.: Cavendish Square, 2019.

Murray, Julie. *New York*. Minneapolis, Minn.: Abdo Publishing, 2020.

Ventura, Marne. *New York City*. Minneapolis, Minn.: Abdo Publishing, 2020.

ON THE WEB

FACTSURFER

Factsurfer.com gives you a safe, fun way to find more information.

1. Go to www.factsurfer.com.

2. Enter "New York" into the search box and click 🔍.

3. Select your book cover to see a list of related content.

INDEX

The images in this book are reproduced through the courtesy of: IM_photo, front cover, pp. 2-3; Luciano Mortula - LGM, pp. 3, 17 (bottom); James Schwabel/ Alamy, pp. 4-5; TTstudio, p. 5 (Empire State Building); Jim Vallee, p. 5 (Letchworth State Park); AG-PHOTOS, p. 5 (Statue of Liberty); Felix Lipov, pp. 5 (Thousand Islands), 10; North Wind Picture Archives/ Alamy, p. 8; pavel TaraSYUK, p. 9; Songquan Deng, p. 11 (top); Colin D. Young, p. 11 (bottom); Steve Byland, pp. 12 (Eastern bluebird), 20 (Eastern bluebird); Warren Metcalf, p. 12 (North American porcupine); Avalon.red/ Alamy, p. 12 (northern flying squirrel); Andrea J Smith, p. 12 (snapping turtle); John Cancalosi/ Alamy, p. 13; Richard Cavalleri, p. 14; Sean Nel, p. 15 (top); Featureflash Photo Agency, p. 15 (middle); ThreeRivers11, p. 15 (bottom); Venturelli Luca, p. 16; GagliardiPhotography, p. 17 (top); littlenySTOCK, p. 18; Winai Tepsuttinun, p. 19 (modern air conditioner); Julie Clopper, p. 19 (Jell-O); Trevor Chriss/ Alamy, p. 19 (Scrabble); exopixel, p. 19 (serrated knife); Alan Budman, p. 19; Brent Hofacker, pp. 20, 21 (tomato pie, egg cream top, egg cream bottom); Dmitrii Ivanov, p. 21 (falafel); TRphotos, p. 22 (top); Roger Cracknell 01/classic/ Alamy, p. 22 (bottom); Allen.G, p. 23 (top); dpa picture alliance/ Alamy, p. 23 (middle); Maks Narodenko, p. 23 (bottom); UPI/ Alamy, pp. 24, 27 (bottom); Inspired By Maps, p. 25; THONGCHAI.S, pp. 26-32; Encyclopedia Britannica, Inc. p. 26 (top); Travel Stock, p. 26 (bottom); Beth Dixson/ Alamy, p. 27 (top); SERGEI BRIK, p. 29 (North American beaver); TJ Brown, p. 29 (rose); Edward Fielding, p. 29 (sugar maple); Kristi Blokhin, p. 31.